Expected to Speak?   Obligated to Speak?

60 MINUTES

TO BETTER

PUBLIC SPEAKING

KEVIN ABDULRAHMAN

"PUBLIC SPEAKING COACH TO THE STARS"

i

ISBN: 978-0-9864542-1-9

Most people don't claim

Quick Results.

I Do.

ABOUT THE AUTHOR

Public Speaking Coach to the stars.

Kevin Abdulrahman's long list of clients include Actors, Associates, Ambassadors, Board Members, CEOs, Delegates, Executives, Entrepreneurs, Senior Managers, Thought Leaders, Partners, Presidents & Royalties.

FOREWORD

The best investment you could ever make is to invest in yourself.

As an international speaker and ambassador myself, I can tell you that the importance of speaking with impact is undeniable.

I've known Kevin for a number of years. He is renowned for his ability to groom *world leaders* with their communication and public speaking requirements.

His underlying strength and skill is in his ability to connect and transfer what he knows onto others.

I enjoyed reading this book since Kevin has always been good at making his public speaking teachings fun and on point. In one of his chapters, he talks about *'painting the picture'*, and from personal experience, I can tell you that this idea alone has made a huge difference to the speeches I give to my audiences from all around the world.

The greatest individuals, professionals and leaders are often remembered because of their ability to speak with impact.

Gone are the days where you could hide behind the desk.

If you want to be taken seriously, get funding for a project, persuade your team members, lead with influence and speak to be heard, you need to polish your public speaking skills.

In this day and age, you will find yourself either being expected to speak, or obligated to speak. As Kevin mentions, *you can't escape public speaking.*

Kevin has taken a serious (and dreaded) subject, and delivered an easy to read (and implement) guide. Anyone can get better, deliver better and feel better- in 60 minutes.

Such is Kevin's command on the subject of public speaking that he was able to convey a significant matter, simply.

That on its own speaks volume.

When you read this book, you will know what I mean.

If you are in need of a speedy guide to speaking better and are pressed for time, this book is for you.

60 minutes is all you'll need to get better at public speaking.

Note my words. This will be one of the best investments you could ever make in your lifetime.

His Excellency Sheikh Mohammed Bin Abdullah Al Thani,
"The First Qatari to Summit Everest"

DEDICATION

Only you can bring out the true value of the written words.

Learn, apply, and forever continue to craft your ability to speak.

You're a part of this book as much as this book shall become a part of you

ACKNOWLEDGMENTS

This book is a labor of love. Distilled drops from tens of thousands of hours spent working with some of the most powerful figures, thought leaders and inspiring minds around the world.

To name you all would require a book of its own. I'm eternally indebted and thankful to the time we have spent, and continue to spend together.

You are the inspiration and sum total of what the book offers today.

For this concept to work, a lengthy elimination process was required.

Much had to go in order to allow for the most applicable techniques to stay.

WHAT IS PUBLIC SPEAKING?

If you intend to communicate a specific message to a group and achieve a desired outcome, you are speaking in public, therefore, public speaking.

Whether you want to influence boardroom members, lead a staff meeting, address your association, represent your company as an ambassador, deliver a sermon, present your project, you are required to stand up and speak.

In this competitive world, savvy and successful individuals know that their ability to speak is a *critical* skill.

Some realize this sooner, others, later.

Everyone reaches the same conclusion- there is no escaping Public Speaking.

Public speaking is a must for any individual, professional, leader- whatever you're into.

There is a demand on every individual and at every level to communicate, effectively.

I've been around the block a few times.

I've witnessed far too many individuals stand up and speak poorly. Some cancel their opportunity to speak and succeed, while others go as far as booking themselves away on the exact dates that they are needed, all in order to avoid having to speak for as little as two minutes.

Perhaps you have disregarded public speaking as something that you could live without. Or maybe like many today, you're so focused with your work that up until now, this skill has been overlooked.

You are not alone.

The majority of people are uncomfortable with their public speaking ability.

They believe they can do better.

The challenges of public speaking isn't something you can sleep through, slip around or hope for it to just go away. It won't.

So, it's best that we deal with it in the simplest and most effect style any challenge is dealt with, and conquered - head on.

"The only way out of a problem

is to go through it"

Anonymous

WHAT'S YOUR REALITY?

i)   You never thought about public speaking.
ii) You've been busy and never got around to it.
iii) You've bought plenty of books but never read them.
iv) You're in a position where people expect you to speak.
v)   You have an obligation to speak. You can't back out of this.
vi) You want to become a great public speaker.

Today our consulting contracts with private companies and public organizations has the bulk of it dedicated to communication training across all levels.

Top teams want *all* their people, from sales reps and mid-level managers to their C level execs, board members and Presidents to Speak with *impact.*

Why? Because,

Your ability to present with power and speak with impact will reflect on how your audience will perceive *you*, your value, your products, your services, your company, your brand, and ultimately your credibility and competence.

But you KNOW this already!

ON A SCALE OF 1 TO 10

HOW DO YOU FEEL ABOUT YOUR PUBLIC SPEAKING ABILITY?

1   2   3   4   5   6   7   8   9   10

Not too confident   Complete Confidence

(If 10, you shouldn't be
reading this book)

"All the great speakers were

bad speakers at first"

Ralph Waldo Emerson

PREFACE

I wrote this book with no regards to publishers, distributors or retailers.

It's just for you, the person that wants to get better at public speaking.

As the comedian Tina Fey wrote of what she picked up from her 'Saturday Night Live' boss, Lorne Michaels, "The show doesn't go on because it's ready; it goes on because it's *eleven thirty*."

You are looking for something concise and comprehensive.

You have picked this book up for a specific reason.

60 minutes is all you've got.

You are in a 'fast and furious' head space, having left your talk/presentation/public address to the last minute.

Yet need to make an impact.

You want some powerful thoughts and techniques to execute immediately.

I've worked hard to make sure that every word included (and the tens of thousands discarded) would genuinely help you with your public speaking *immediately.*

I've pieced the book together for you to use as a reference (survive and thrive) every time you need to get up and speak.

I want you to *enjoy* public speaking like I have taught thousands of other in my seminars around the world to do so- in a disarming and relaxed manner.

The thoughts and techniques are *simple* to implement, yet *significant* in the difference it will bring to your results.

If you feel you are closing on to eleven thirty, rest assured, *I got you!*

60 minutes to better public speaking will help you become a better public speaker.

That's my promise.

These techniques have worked with Presidents.

It will work for you.

Your 60 minutes starts NOW!

1 LISTEN TO MAMA

You may feel uncomfortable at the thought of having to speak.

Anxious, stressed, tensed, a stiff neck, croaky throat, dry mouth, perhaps even considering calling in sick (I've seen it happen far too many times) because of an upcoming speaking engagement.

Mama always told me this as a kid,

"Kevin stop. Take ten deep and slow breaths. 10, 9 , 8, 7, 6, 5, 4, 3, 2, 1. Okay, now go and take on the world".

I know what you are thinking.

I thought the same.

What does breathing have to with getting rid of my speaking nerves?

Without getting into too much science, when you stop and take in ten long and deep breaths, you fill your lungs and brain with more oxygen.

You will also sense everything slow down (like you see in the movies) and begin to feel relaxed.

Make sure that you breathe in fully, filling up your diaphragm (area just under your rib cage). A good deep breath should have your stomach pop out like you have swallowed an entire week's dinner in one sitting.

My mama is now your mama, which means we have to listen to her.

Take ten deep breaths.

It will take you less than 2 minutes.

Two minutes that will make all the difference.

"Sky above me, earth below me,
fire within me."

SKYRIM

2 THE SECRET IS OUT

I've helped tens of thousands of clients from all walks of life by sharing with them a secret.

Would you like to know what it is?

Come closer, so I can tell you what I tell them.

Have *fun*.

You're saying, "Kevin I'm an intellectual. I have to speak about something that falls in the boring but important category"

I will still tell you the same thing – Have fun.

Most people, including yourself have forgotten about this innate ability and desire of humans to have fun.

You perform your best when you're are having fun, and frankly, I don't care how serious you may have grown to become, you know how to have fun. At least at some point in your life you did.

Tell me, when was the last time you attended a talk, training, media press, trade event or conference with the voluntary intention of *being bored of your brains*?

You didn't.

Believe me then when I say that your audience (whatever the case maybe) are no different than you and I.

They don't want to be dulled and lulled into a coma.

They would *love* to enjoy and be engaged when hearing you speak (even about a serious topic).

Having fun is an attitude.

When you choose this attitude, you will learn more, strive to refine your thoughts, pull together your best work, polish your public speaking skills even further and boldly take on every opportunity you get to present.

When you're having fun, your audience will be much more receptive to your thoughts, ideas and suggestions.

When you're having fun, your audience will see you as charismatic, comfortable, confident and commanding.

Now tell me you don't want all that?

Of course you do.

3 IT AIN'T SO BAD

Here's another question I ask my clients.

What's the worst that can happen as a result of your public speaking?

I want you to write this down.

_____

_____

In most cases, everyone gets to live another day.

If it isn't, reading this book is an unrealistic outcome for what you need.

If it's not life threatening, relax.

"Even if you fall on

your face, you're still

moving forward"

Robert Gallagher

4 JUST A THOUGHT

You may be concerned with what your audience will think, when you stand up to deliver your message.

Let me tell you what they won't be thinking.
 "hahaha look at him/her. She is so nervous. Sucker."

What they will be thinking (99.99% of the time) is,
"Geee Wizzz, I'm glad it's not me standing up there".

"If you're going through hell, keep going"

Winston Churchill

5 FRAME IT RIGHT

When asked to deliver a talk, many individuals often speak about how great they are, what their company is all about and the amazing line up of products or services they can offer.

STOP!!!

You may be speaking, but avoid making the mistake of delivering a talk that is framed around you (and what you represent).

Your entire message needs to be framed around a simple life principle 'WIIFM' – What's In It For Me.

Every time you are crafting your message, ask yourself, "What's in it for my audience"?

If you have a sales background then you will know that people don't buy features (wrong frame).

They buy benefits (right frame).

It isn't about how great you or your group is, it's about how the audience can benefit from what you have to offer.

Always account for this critical element.

Frame it before you Phrase it.

"The goal of effective communication should be for listeners to say 'Me too!' versus 'So what?'"

Jim Rohn

6 FEAR AND YOU

Some common fears most people experience about public speaking:

Fear of the unknown

Fear of rejection

Fear of looking stupid

Fear of exclusion

Fear of past mishap

Fear of getting it wrong

Fear of blacking out

Fear of looking incompetent

Fear of looking unnatural

Fear of not being liked or loved

Apply what I share with you in this book, and every one of those fears will dissipate into thin air.

Your past is not your future.

So what if you make a mistake when you get up and speak?

It happens to the best of us.

All these fears stem from past experiences, other people's experiences and an incorrect point of reference- *you*.

Let's deal with it.

"I must not fear.

Fear is the mind-killer. Fear is the little death that brings total obliteration.

I will face my fear.

I will permit it to pass over me and through me. And when it has gone past, I will turn the inner eye to see its path.

Where the fear has gone, there will be nothing.

Only I will remain."

Frank Herber

7 WHY SO SERIOUS?

So you have to deliver a talk?

Why so serious?

If you are ever anxious, then you've got things mixed up.

You think it's about you.

Newsflash! It's *not* about you.

It's about the audience.

Your role is to deliver a message.

Your role is to care for your audience.

Care enough to ensure your audience receives the intended message.

Ever walked down the street and experienced a complete stranger giving you a smile?

In most cases, the most natural and instinctive response would be to smile back.

There is a human law, powerful in the outcome it provides, simple in its application.

The law of *reciprocity* has it that we as humans are inclined to reciprocate what we receive.

People don't care how much you know until *they know how much you care.*

We like those who like us.

We love those who love us.

We care for those that care for us.

You'd have to work pretty hard to find someone you like that dislikes you. If you do, congratulations, but there aren't that many of them.

Care for your audience.

They will see it, appreciate it and as a result reciprocate this feeling by caring and listening to you.

8 RE-LABEL YOUR FEELINGS

Think of the first time you went on a date.

Excited. Nervous. Anxious. Heart pounding. Butterflies. Some or all of the above.

But you labelled it *positive*!

You control the label you give your feelings. Every time.

Public speaking is no different. Re-label your feelings.

Useless labels	New Positive Label
Anxious?	Good. You're alive
Freaking out	Excited
Nervous	You're a rock star. Your job is to do your best..
Fearful	So is having a baby. But a lot of fun.
Sleepless	Good. More time to practice.

The best speakers use mind games.

It works for them.

It will work for you.

"Turn your face to the sun and the shadows fall behind you"

Maori Proverb

9 SIZE UP YOUR COMPETITION

If this was a boxing ring, you are facing off against a competitor who is undefeated, has twice your reach, three times your size, and oh, I nearly forgot, is considered to be the world champion. Good luck!

Fair to say, you won't be winning this match.

Good news. You aren't in a boxing ring.

Bad news. Your competitor is far more fierce than what I described.

When speaking, you are facing off against what is still deemed to be the most powerful machine in the history of mankind.

You are not dealing with a smart phone or a tablet.

You are dealing with the mighty *mind*.

Most people speak, on average, between 120-180 words a minute. A turtle like speed when comparing it to the 400+ words a minute the brain can process.

Meaning: If you deliver a boring, standard or weak performance, within minutes, the two of you (you speaking and your audience's mind) will be miles apart.

"The single biggest problem in communication is the *illusion* that it has taken place"

George Bernard Shaw

And if that wasn't enough, I've got more bad news for you.

A.D.D used to be described as a clinical term to label the restless few.

Thanks to the beeps, tweets, pings, rings and mental dings, I say that everyone today suffers from A.D.D (yours truly being right at the top of that list)

How's that for a brutal match?

Solution:

Be Sharp.

Be on point.

How?

Read on.

10 DRAW THE FINISH LINE

The chances are you're an expert in what you will be speaking on.

This means that you can probably speak for weeks on end about your topic.

Intuitively, you're thinking, *great*.

Nope. That's not the case.

Your audience won't give you minutes of their time, let alone an entire week.

Your audience is preoccupied with other pressing issues in life.

They don't have time for blabber.

If you are *off point,* you won't even get a minute.

Most people consider crafting their message from a starting point.

It may sound right. But it's not.

Two significant questions are unanswered, resulting in individuals finding themselves frustrated and completely off course from their audience. The problem- there is no end in mind.

You must first start by drawing your finish line.

Answer these two questions,

What's the purpose of you standing up to speak?

_____

What do you want the audience to remember (or do) after having heard you speak?

_____

Understand, you may find it difficult to articulate a valid answer at first. But you *must* press yourself to get a crystal clear answer.

This is the focal point from which you establish a clear sense of direction.

Consider this. You are about to leave your office and get into your car. The question you would have had to successfully answer at some point prior to driving away would have been a variation of *"what destination am I driving to?"*

So, I ask you to pose the same question about your talk.

Where are you driving to with your talk?

What destination are you driving your audience to?

Only once you've established a finish line, you start.

11 LET IT STORM

Go nuts.

Write *all* your thoughts on paper.

Write all over the place.

Write even if it does not make any sense.

Write without editing.

Write freely.

Write in abundance.

Write like you will gain a second life time.

Write all the things that come to mind.

If time permits, take a break. Perhaps when you are doing the groceries later in the day more will come. It always does. Come back, and write.

Write until you're exhausted.

When outlining and writing out your talk or speech, you have my permission to Brainstorm freely.

This is the place and perhaps the only time you will exercise your freedom to put down any gibberish.

Beware: Most professionals deliver their talks at this stage and wonder why their audience have glazy eyes and fallen into a coma.

YOU WILL NEVER DO THIS.

"Every speaker has a mouth;
An arrangement rather neat.
Sometimes it's filled with wisdom.
Sometimes it's filled with feet."

Robert Orben

12 A PAINFUL PROCESS

Once you go through brainstorming all the great ideas, thoughts, stories, analogies and examples, comes the process of filtering.

It starts of as fun at the beginning, but the more you have to remove, the more painful the process becomes.

If it is in line with your purpose, it stays.

If it's not. Cut.

Everybody thinks their thoughts are great (and they could be), but your audience's mind is *merciless*.

Unfortunately, you don't have the luxury to be emotional about your content.

If you bore or confuse your audience, they will disregard your message.

No second chances.

This book was originally 500+ pages (already edited).

Imagine the cruelty endured to deliver a 60 minutes condensed version.

If I am to speak ten minutes, I need a
week for preparation;

if fifteen minutes, three days;

if half an hour, two days;

if an hour, I am ready now.

Woodrow Wilson

Realize, the shorter the time you have to deliver your message, the harder you *will* have to work.

Now I've got you thinking.

"What must stay? What must go?"

Thought you'd never ask.

13 SHOULD I STAY OR SHOULD I GO?

You will be faced with removing great bits and pieces.

The questions you need to ask are

1. What is the purpose of standing up to speak?
2. Is this point in line with the outcome I would like to achieve?
3. Does it fit?
4. Does it flow? (I'll touch on this shortly)

In many cases, when working with clients, we removed so much great material that they used the discarded content to prepare a couple of different speeches from it. They stashed it in their content reserve bank for future use. You can do the same.

Sometimes your facts, thoughts and ideas may look great at first, but then it just doesn't sound right. Or it may not fit with your outcome.

What do you do?

Delete.

Keep removing every bit of excess fat from the body, until the piece, presentation, pitch or public address becomes a lean mean muscular machine that is ready to take on the fierce competition.

"If you can't explain it simply, you don't understand it well enough."

Albert Einstein

14 EDWARD WHO?

Edward Everett is rarely remembered as a keynote speaker.

Do you remember him?

Don't be concerned. Over the years, only about 5% of my seminar attendees have heard of him.

In 1863, Edward was a keynote speaker. He spoke for over two hours.

So what's so special about not remembering Edward and his two hour speech?

Because you've probably heard of the other guy that spoke after him - Abraham Lincoln.

He *wasn't* the keynote speaker on that day.

He didn't have the two hours Edward Everett had.

Yet, to this very day, Abraham Lincoln is remembered for delivering the iconic *Gettysburg Address*.

The length of his speech?

Two minutes. 10 sentences. 272 words.

15 GET THEIR ATTENTION

"Good afternoon ladies and gentlemen.

Thank you for coming. Today I will...."

Start with this, and the subconscious mind of your audience is given the cue (because they already know what's coming from their agonizing experience)

a. This is going to be BORING!!!
b. Why am I here? I have so much work to catch up on.
c. Who looks more comfortable? Should I lean to the left or right to fall asleep.

You have lost the match with your introduction.

If you can't captivate your audience at the beginning, you have no chance of delivering a great message (no matter how good you are).

People today are mentally occupied, stretched and exhausted.

Your audience will usually be (and don't take this personally) absent minded, stressed about their work load, traumatized by mounting emails, the kids, what to cook for dinner, you get the picture.

What they don't need is another person trying to take up space in their head.

If you go in like everyone else does, you are singing a lullaby – *Hello Coma!*

You might be speaking to a full house. Realize it's only a full house of bodies.

The house is mentally empty.

Your job is to bring the audience mentally into the room.

Get their attention.

"How do you do that?", I hear you asking.

"Smooth seas don't make skillful sailors"

African proverb

16 START DIFFERENT

"I think my career just peaked" was Colin Firth's first words when accepting the Oscar for his deserving role in The King's Speech.

You could state a startling fact that might not be commonly known to get people's attention. For example, you might be in the aviation sector and are required to speak on a particular aspect- safety.

"Did you know that the likelihood of a fatality is 8 times greater when driving than when flying?"

Your topic may be boring.

Your topic may be important.

But you have no right to use them as reasons for numbing your audience.

Get Creative.

Start from the middle of the room.

Start from the back.

Start by highlighting a dilemma.

Start with a fact.

Start with impact.

Start with a quote.

Share an anecdote.

Start with a distraction (but relevant to a point you are making).

Share and show your point through an action.

Imagine turning up to an event and the speaker for that evening decided to walk in wearing his Pyjamas.

(if you haven't already seen it, go online and Google 'Leadership Speaker Pyjamas')

Arouse your audience's mind.

Get their attention, or you're better off going home.

"Anyone who trades liberty for security deserves neither"

Benjamin Franklin

17 THAT DON'T IMPRESS ME MUCH

All too often, talks and public addresses go wrong because the speaker thinks this is the time to stroke their own ego.

I've seen professionals misuse their speaking time to show off their capabilities, vocabulary of lingos, complex scenarios and fancy presentations.

They talk so much gibberish, supposedly to suggest they are smart.

Let me tell you, there is nothing smart about this approach.

All it does is detract away from your *purpose* as a speaker.

Your endgame isn't to impress your audience

Your purpose is to *deliver* your message.

Do this and your audience will be impressed.

This may be 'show time' for you, but it is *not* the time to show off.

This is the time (a very limited one) for you to deliver your intended message with clarity, purpose and impact.

Don't talk gibberish.

Don't use lingo (unless it's a crowd completely made up of people who speak the lingo).

The vocabulary you use shouldn't be designed to impress people (you should be a rapper if you want otherwise) .

Don't get fancy.

Keep it simple.

Deliver your message with the simplicity of delivering it to a 9-10 year old kid.

Like all great speakers, Winston Churchill, understood the power of simplicity.

When delivering his famous October speech in 1941, he picked a key message and delivered it,

"Never Give In. Never Give In. Never. Never. Never"

A key message repeated over and over again.

Sharp.

On point.

That's how you deliver with impact.

You *will* be impressive.

"Think like a wise man but communicate in the language of the people."

William Butler Yeats

18 LET IT FLOW

Ever stared at a river?

It just flows. Effortless. Beautiful.

When you stand up to deliver, I want you think of your message like a river. The flow of information must make effortless sense.

I've seen people get up and speak an insane amount of nonsense, with an expectation that their audience will somehow make sense of it.

Wake up!

If it doesn't make sense to you, then it won't make sense to your audience.

If it's hazy in your mind, it will be a sandstorm in the minds of your audience.

If your audience have to think about it, you've lost them.

The last thing you want is an audience that's trying to figure out what you have just said.

They will *stop* listening. Period.

Your audience don't have the chance to question what you really mean?

Your audience don't have time to think about what you are saying.

Re-read the above line until it sinks in.

Say what you mean. Mean what you say.

Your talk needs to be one that is *easy* on the minds of your audience.

I'm not demeaning the audience.

They are smart. They are also mentally lazy.

They just don't want to think or have to think.

They need to be able to follow you with absolute ease.

You are the one standing.

You are the one delivering.

You are responsible that your message makes sense. Not the audience.

Remember that a river flows effortlessly.

Does your river of information flow?

"He who wants to persuade should put his trust, not in the right argument, but in the right word"

Joseph Conrad

19 BRING IT TO LIFE

Too many professionals stand up and deliver their message crammed with facts and figures.

They assume the audience to be logical creatures.

Sorry. I hate to be breaking it to you, but we are emotional creatures. We prefer vivid visuals over numbing numbers.

If you want to deliver facts with impact, you need to paint the picture in the minds of the audience.

Help your audience *realize* what you mean.

Fact: *"Burj Khalifa is the tallest tower in the world at 828m"*

The statement states a fact. But it's just a number.

It doesn't come close to painting a picture and perhaps saying,

"Burj Khalifa is the tallest tower in the world. At 828m, it is the size of eight football fields stacked up on top of each other"

You are the painter, and your audience's mind is a blank canvas.

Evoke their emotions. Explore their senses.

Give your message color. Give it shade.

Give it depth. Give it dimension.

Give it taste. Give it flavor.

Give it feel. Give it texture.

Your audience can only see what you see, but only after you do a good job of painting the picture for them.

"I dream of painting and then
I paint my dream"

Vincent Van Gogh

20 PROJECT POWER

Umms, ahhhs, like, you know, OK, actually...

Don't even think about it.

There is power in pausing.

Silence is uncomfortable for most people.

Use it as your power play.

Your ability to have a moment of pause without using gap fillers will help you exude *confidence*.

You will be seen as someone that's *comfortable*, and in *command*.

Pausing allows your audience to take in and think about what you just said.

Pausing will have your audience hanging on a cliff waiting for you to deliver your statement with impact.

Pausing is the punctuation you would otherwise use if you were communicating in writing to your reader.

Pausing gives you poise.

And to be absolutely frank, pausing buys you a couple of seconds to gather yourself (if you've lost your train of thought) and deliver your next point, with power.

You get the idea.

Pause.

"Well-timed silence hath more eloquence than speech"

Martin Fraquhar Tupper

21 SHORT AND SNAPPY

With everything you've learned so far, revisit your talk.

Consider every point.

Ask yourself, *"How can I clean this up? Make it shorter? Make it punchier?"*

When speaking, your statements should only ever be long by necessity, not by choice.

Do you want to considered in the same breath of great orators, thought leaders and Presidents?

You can.

Here's how the most powerful speakers win their audience over.

They use

    a. Short sentences
    b. Simple words
    c. Terms that everyone can identify and relate to

Quality over quantity.

Less is more.

"A good speech should be like a woman's skirt; long enough to cover the subject and short enough to create interest."

Anonymous

22 PRESIDENTIAL CLOSE

People remember the *first* and *last* thing you say.

If your audience were interviewed and asked, what one point did they remember about your message, what would it be?

What's the summary and reason for why you stood up to speak?

What's your drive home message?

The close is where you are mentally rallying your audience to action.

What is your call for action?

Bring it home.

Follow the public speaking axiom – *"Have a powerful, captivating opening and a strong, memorable close, and put the two of them as close together as possible."*

Note: If you have the time to practice, check out the last two minutes of some your favorite (well spoken) politicians campaigning. Their close should help you *realize* their message and call for action.

End on a high note.

End with hope.

End with a smile.

End with poise.

End with power.

Your last words are remembered, make them count.

"Yes We Can!"

Barack Obama

Campaign slogan, 2008

23 YOU'RE BETTER THAN YOU THINK

I Believe it.

Now I just need to show and make you believe it too.

First of all, believe in that there is a reason why you have been asked to speak. There is *value* in what you have to share with the audience.

You better believe it.

"If you think you can, and if you think you can't, then you are probably right"

Henry Ford

Secondly, just so you don't think I'm a motivational *raaa raaa raaa* kind of speaker, let me give you this reality to help bolster your belief in yourself.

Take any recording device (laptop, smart phone or camcorder if you still use one) and record yourself delivering your talk.

You will

    a)   Become aware of the areas you need to fine tune.

    b)   Realize what I help many of my clients appreciate when running group workshops or one on one trainings. As in every case I've worked on, you'll notice that you come across a lot better than you think.

Now go record, watch and surprise yourself with the trial.

I know, I know. You can buy me a coffee when we meet. I Love you too.

24 STAND TALL

From when you walk into the room, or even getting out of your car, the moment you're spotted, it's *game on*.

Your posture (standing tall) portrays that you are confident and in command.

You must walk and ultimately stand with poise.

How you come across is the texture you give to what you say.

When speaking, stand with your legs hip distant apart. Enough to hold your balance. You don't want to be wobbling from side to side or rocking back and forth.

Your shoulders pushed back with your head centered, looking at the audience

You are standing tall.

Your airways are open for you to breathe and speak with ease.

This is a winner's posture.

You establish authority, are in control and look both comfortable and competent.

Look the part.

Be the part.

Stand tall.

"A good stance and posture reflect a proper state of mind."

Morihei Ueshiba

25 DIASRM AND CONNECT

Did you know, kids smile over 400 times, a day?

That number is reduced to an average of only 15 a day as adults.

When it comes to public speaking, the average goes down to just a handful, and I'm being generous.

Far too many individuals are great when I meet with them one on one.

Then, they stand up to speak.

Suddenly, they look constipated (not a pretty sight).

Let me tell you something.

Before ability, comes *likeability*.

A plain, grumpy or constipated face doesn't constitute likeability.

Humans gravitate to a natural smile

We feel good when we smile (or witness it on others).

Before you have a chance to demonstrate your ability, you must win your audience over. Smiling gives you likeability.

Likeability gives you a *listening* audience.

You can tell your audience that you are happy to see them, be with them, and share your message. But you have to let your face know about it.

You can say all of that with a genuine and heartfelt smile.

Understand, your facial expression must be in line with what you are saying. Unless you're delivering a eulogy or are dealing with the media in a crisis management mode, smiling is the fastest way to disarm and connect with your audience.

It is up to you to apply it depending on the context of when, where and why you are speaking.

It doesn't cost you anything to smile, but it buys you immeasurable goodwill.

You will get the majority of your audience from the get go.

Smiling is a weapon. Use it.

"Your smile is a messenger of

your goodwill"

Dale Carnegie

26 MOVE WITH PURPOSE

Don't just stand behind the lectern (unless you're delivering a public address broadcasted to the entire world)

Don't hide behind objects. They won't save you.

Don't move without purpose. Your audience will leave scared and scarred.

Don't wonder and wobble. They'll call the paramedics.

Don't be glued to one spot. You'll blend in with the furniture.

Remember, your audience don't have much of an attention span.

Once you get their attention at the start, you have to continuously keep their attention.

You need to engage them with everything you've got.

Use the space you have.

Depending on the situation, you may be able to only move across one dimension (such as a stage), in which case you have *left, center and right.*

If in a room, you could utilize the entire room.

Move. But only do so with purpose.

Make a move to one side of the room and deliver your point.

You can then signal your next point by making the next move.

This will engage your audience, help you cover the room, and more importantly aid you in delivering your message with impact.

Far better than a stiff 'behind the lectern' type of speaker, don't you agree?

"You can have brilliant ideas, but if you can't get them across, your ideas won't get you anywhere."

Lee Iacocca

27 SIGN LANGUAGE

Gestures are imperative to convey your message. Again, with purpose.

Don't flap your arms like you are having a seizure or attempting to land 3 flies in one scoop.

Keep your arms above your waist.

Your gestures is sign language. It needs to be *in line* with your message.

Your hands should move, only when a point is made.

If you are saying it's *big*, ensure that your gestures reflect 'big' and not otherwise.

I beg you, please don't do something because you saw a public figure do it.

The *power pose* is a power pose for those who pull it off naturally. It is not a pose you hold for ten minutes because you *think* it exudes power.

Not only will you look like a gimp, you will also come across as *fake*.

Your audience don't want fake. They want an authentic speaker.

Authenticity is what gets you respect from your audience.

You want to come across as powerful?

Take a few gestures from the likes of presidents and great orators, see which one works with your personality, and then use them as part of your repertoire. You may want to go for Obama's *C hand gesture* or Donald Trump's use of the *steeple*.

Whatever you choose, it must seem natural for you.

"Nothing hinders a thing from being natural so much as straining ourselves to make it seem so."

Francois de La Rochefoucauld

28 BE MAGNETIC

They are alluring. They are charismatic. They are charming. They are enigmatic. They have an undeniable presence.

They have a way about them.

They command attention.

These are but some of the attractive qualities people notice in great orators.

How would you like to become more charismatic?

How would you like to command presence?

What if you could be Magnetic?

Easy.

Look up. Make eye contact.

Many make the mistake of standing up and looking down.

Others look at everything except for the one place that matters – *the audience.*

I know you might be thinking, *"But Kevin, it's overwhelming to look up at an audience of 5,50,500 or 5000 people".*

Relax. We are going to re-label it.

You are not giving a talk to five hundred people.

You are speaking *one on one*, five hundred times.

Break the audience down mentally into 6 segments, depending on the setting.

Back Left	*Center*	*Back Right*
Front Left	*Center*	*Front Right*

Every time you make a point, look in the direction of one of these segments.

More importantly, look for a face that is engaged with what you are saying.

Look them in the eye and deliver your point.

Speak as you would speak to them, one on one.

When it's time to make your next point, look towards another segment, pick a face, look them in the eye and deliver your point.

You will find yourself going through the segments a few times and every time you would have had a one on one conversation with someone in the audience.

Suddenly your rounds of one on ones add up to a good chunk of your audience

Benefit:

You make one on one connections.

You create admiring fans within your audience.

You helped work the audience to feel engaged and involved.

Make one on one connections by looking people in the eye, holding your gaze (in a gentle non-creepy manner) as you make your point.

The eyes are indeed the *windows to the soul* and when you do this in a disarming manner, your audience would have looked right into you and sensed your authenticity.

They will find you magnetic, and you will feel it.

29 THE VOICE

You want to be heard.

You want to be understood.

You want your message to be delivered with clarity.

Your ability to speak with a voice that projects authority, confidence, enthusiasm and magnitude adds weight to the content of what you are saying.

This desire however, results in a common blunder- individuals speaking really loud.

They want their message to reach, so they *scream*.

"The less people know,

the more they yell."

Seth Godin

Screaming your message won't serve you. It will hurt your audience's ears and detract from the message you intend to deliver.

Note: speaking too softly will also detract your audience's attention. Instead of listening to your message, they will be hedging bets with one another trying to figure out the words you're mumbling.

You want a commanding voice.

You want a clear voice.

You want an authentic voice- your voice.

Implementing vocal variety will help you in emphasizing key points.

Happiness, sadness, empathy, passion- all can be conveyed with your voice.

Imagine *what you say* as outlining pictures in the audience's mind. You have then shaded it in with your posture, movement and gestures. Your voice is what gives color and life to these pictures (*how you say it*).

As soon as we begin working together, I tell clients to stop using their *lazy posture voice*. You know, the posture (and resulting voice) you have after a long day.

You are drooping and feel like doing nothing more than drag yourself from the ground and onto a couch.

No shallow speaking (using only the air in your mouth)

You want and need a strong voice, that comes from your core.

Place your hand just below your rib cage and feel yourself taking in deep breaths expanding your diaphragm. This should have your hand move forward and backwards (not up and down).

Remember Mama's lesson? Ten deep breaths, then begin speaking.

Pay special attention that you project your voice from your diaphragm.

It will feel odd at first, but this is your *real voice*- your authentic voice.

With practice, you will captivate your audience with your authentic voice.

You will have an amazing feeling of authority, control and peace, speaking from such depth.

Your audience will hear and experience a remarkable difference.

Welcome to the voice of your future.

30 I WANT TO BE OBAMA

No you don't (even though it's undeniable, Obama is a great orator)

But you really don't.

Ok, I'll be the guy that breaks your heart (tough love) and just say it.

You will *never* be Obama.

If it makes you feel better - Obama can never be you either.

The mistake many make (and you see this with girls that wreck themselves with bad plastic surgeries) is that they want to be someone else.

You can't be anyone but yourself.

Don't start a fight you're sure to lose.

The best you could ever come close to is be *'like Obama'*. And being *like* someone is not a compliment.

You can't be better (or beat) someone else at being them and neither will they at bettering you.

You can only become the best that you can be.

Use the likes of Obama as inspiration, not imitation.

Be You.

Do You.

31 BLACK OUT

What if you are up there speaking and suddenly black out?

Don't worry. It happens.

> "The human brain starts working the moment you are born and never stops until you stand up to speak in public"
>
> George Jessel

I'll give you two quick techniques that will serve you forever when speaking in public.

    a)   First technique is the use of *triggers*.

Within the flow of your storyline, *triggers will* help you recall and connect your points together. You can use either or all of the following techniques to help deliver with impact.

    i)   Delivering your points by listing them (1. 2. 3. 4. 5.).

    ii)   Stories with turning points (highs and lows, mentally leading you onto the next scene)

iii) The use of your fingers (this is listing in a physical form to help with thought recollection).

iv) Body movement (Certain points and aligned movements in your storyline will bring about the vision of what comes next).

b) The second technique is what we've covered, *re-labelling*.

Re-label your audience from *arch enemies* to *friends.*

You are amongst friends.

What are friends for?

Think of them as saying, in the words of Jerry McGuire , *"Help me, Help you"*

If you ever black out and have absolutely no idea where you were, *own up to it-* ask your audience to help you.

I do it. And I get paid to speak.

I've repeatedly told my audience, *"You know what, I must be a goldfish, and I must be out of water, because I have no idea what I was saying. Where was I folks?"*

The audience laughs (1 point), they see my authenticity (1 point) and they actively participate in reminding me (and themselves) what I said last (1 point).

Suddenly, you have taken what most people are so afraid of, and turning it to your advantage.

This is the advantage when you see your audience as friends.

Now, where was I? Right ☺

32 MAKE IT A MOVIE

Avoid memorizing.

This may sound counter intuitive since many seasoned professionals will grin with pride by saying that they have memorized their talk, speech or presentation.

You will end up with a loaded brain, and ultimately hinder yourself when it's game time.

If you want to be calm, cool and collected before you get up to speak, *relieve* your brain of any unnecessary load.

Give your message a structure- like a story line for a movie.

Then, like any story or movie, you can visualize and recall the events because it makes *logical* sense.

Think of the last time you caught up with a friend and relived a movie you watched, a holiday you just had, or even how you spent the weekend.

Your story had a start, followed by a series of events and a finish.

It had *flow*.

You may have recalled every little detail, or you may have missed one or two minor things.

But you had flow, from start to finish.

A simple story line can help you visualize and link your thoughts (with the help of triggers) from start to the finish.

Don't memorize your talk. Turn it into a movie.

33 ARRIVE EARLY

Where are you speaking?

Go check out the set up. Get a feel for the place. Have a walk around.

It's amazing how much this move alone can positively affect your overall result.

Whether it's the day earlier or even an hour before hand, having access to where you will be delivering your talk, knowing where you will be standing to speak, seeing the setup, getting a feel for the size of the room/auditorium, doing some sounds checks will all be helpful.

Your mind will store the context, feel and surroundings. When you get to doing the real thing, your mind will consider it to be a familiar place, helping you be more at ease.

Pay close attention to what I'm going to say next.

Arriving early enables you to play as an *unofficial* host, meet with attendees as they come in, chat with them, get on a first name basis and build rapport.

This boosts your likeability in the mind of the people you connect with.

When people like you, they will trust you.

When they trust you, they will listen to you.

The fact that you are taking the time to get to know them will significantly increase the chance of them liking you, trusting you and when it counts, to really hear you out.

"You can't make an omelette without breaking eggs"

Proverb

34 TAILOR MADE

Bring the audience in and make them a part of what you say.

Like a fitted suit, nothing is more alluring than a fitted message.

You'll stand out and look sharp.

Your message will resonate with the audience. They'll feel connected.

Always seek to understand

1. Who your audience is?

2. What is the context? Is there a burning issue?

3. Why are you speaking?

4. What is the expectation from you standing up to speak?

Constantly strive to tailor make your message at every opportunity you get.

Example A: You can make a point to thank your audience that have travelled from a distance to be at the international launch of your product by saying *"Like Tony Gonzales who travelled all the way from Mexico to be with us here in Malaysia, I want to thank every single one of you for taking the time and making the effort to be here with us today. You will love the benefits and edge our new gadget will bring you and your customers"*

Example B: You may be representing your government and delivering a public address at a "green energy" conference which revolves around utilizing the brains of our youth.

On arriving early, you meet with a number of attendees, one of whom is a gentleman in his thirties that's clearly passionate about the topic. He shares with you some of what his team is implementing.

As part of the points you make in an obviously well-crafted and clear talk, you incorporate your conversation as a real life example of the point you are making.

"I believe that we have untapped amounts of energy from natural resources and more importantly from the talent that is all around us. Take for example Khalid, who shared with me some brilliant ideas that he and has team have been working on over the last year. I will certainly be following up with him on that, but I tell you, opportunities and talents are all around us. We simply have to wake up and be active about seeking it."

Remember: We all appreciated tailored items.

35 HANDLE THE ELEPHANT

If there is an elephant in the room, point it out.

Crisis and redundancies? State it.

Facing challenges? State it.

Mistakes made? State it.

A significant day in history, mention it.

Whether it's silly or significant, issues must be handled.

Some years ago, I was on a speaking tour. At a conference in the United Arab Emirates, I delivered a keynote speech to a group. 15 minutes later, the first question I got had nothing to do with my keynote.

The young lady at the back got a microphone and asked, *"where is your accent from?"*.

Because of my background and extensive travel, I'm considered to have somewhat of a funny *no-man's land* accent.

I thought was a small and insignificant aspect. But it wasn't.

It was an elephant that got in the way of my message. A lesson I learned to deal with at the start, prior to delivering my keynote.

Some elephants are bigger than others.

Get in your audience's seat.

Figure out what they would be thinking.

Do they have questions? Concerns?

Don't gloss over things. Handle it in advance.

Warren Buffet's holding company Berkshire Hathaway (whose single share is usually in excess of $100,000) tend to start their yearly report by telling their investors where they have gone wrong along with the challenges experienced. Only then they talk about their results.

If your audience feel an issue must be mentioned, cite it.

If you don't, you are wasting your time.

Your audience won't be hearing you.

They can't.

There is an elephant in the way.

"Intellectuals solve problems,
geniuses prevent them."

Albert Einstein

36 PRACTICE IS OVER-RATED

No it's not.

Once you have structured your message into a flow, practice is an absolute must.

Many years ago, I met with Sir Anthony Hopkins in Sydney. This man's incredible presence in the roles he played didn't just come from turning up to the set unprepared. He would go over the story-line thousands of times. He literally became the characters he was playing. Such was his dedication to the art of acting and speaking.

Now I am not saying that you turn in to character every time (well actually, you should, if you have the time), but realize that the greatest of orators practice tirelessly.

The more practiced you are, the more comfortable, confident and commanding you will be.

The more practice you have under your belt, the more at ease you will be with your message.

Your focus can then shift to deliver with impact.

Everything I shared with you throughout the book will ensure that you practice with ease.

The best political figures and CEOs practice long and hard. They find time between their schedule to fit it in. They do it all day, all night, at lunch breaks, between meetings, walking on the streets, in the bathrooms, literally everywhere. You might even see me walking in your city like a madman talking to myself. It's practice.

Every chance you get, practice.

Practice mentally, physically, visually and vocally.

You can't just read text and call it practice.

It's called public speaking. You have to speak.

Take comedians, they come up with new material and test them out in local bars. They get their feedback by seeing what flies, what doesn't, what needs refining, what needs to be cut out.

When you hear yourself speak, you pick up on what needs changing, how your content flows, what additions and subtractions need to made. It's amazing how much you can self-correct simply by hearing and feeling yourself speak.

If you have the time, call on some friends. Perhaps you have a cat that will have to endure some suffering. If all else fails, call on for some undeniable and credible feedback- the mirror on the wall.

"Don't be afraid to talk to yourself.

It's the only way you can be sure somebody's listening."

F.P. Jones.

37 JUDGEMENT DAY

Never judge a book by its cover.

And yet, we all do it.

Your audience will make a judgment of you, whether you like it or not, whether you're deserving of it or not.

It's your responsibility to win over every single point you can.

Here are a few quick and easy points you *must* score.

This was included because I'm, to this very day, baffled as to why common sense doesn't seem to be so common.

1. Look Good. I shouldn't be saying this but I will. Dress well. Dress for the occasion. Look the part. If in doubt, over dress.

2. Smell good – Again it goes without saying, that we find ourselves liking those who smell good. Have a shower before you are required to go and speak. You need to be clean and fresh. Having bad body odor is uncomfortable and distracting for your audience.

3. Feel good. From head to toe, wear only what makes you

feel comfortable. Don't put on a $300 silk shirt if you're allergic to silk. It doesn't matter how much you paid or how great it looks on camera. You want to look good not like someone trying to scratch off fleas from their chest-*distracting*.

38 TIME'S UP

The audience clapped- *because they wanted him off stage*.

Your audience won't appreciate being told that a sales presentation is 30 minutes for it to end up being 90 minutes, or that a public address will only be 8 minutes and it ends up being 27 minutes.

Stick to time. In fact, finish *before* time.

No one complains when you are under time.

Your audience will appreciate when you finish on or before time.

The feeling you must aspire to leave your audience with is *"I want more"*.

Whether you are doing a *three minutes* business pitch on a TV show, heading a board meeting or speaking on stage, stick to your time.

This is a non-negotiable criteria for your overall image and ultimate results.

Leave your audience wanting more.

"Be sincere, be brief, be seated."

Franklin Roosevelt

39 VISUALIZE SUCCESS

Visualize delivering a great talk.

Visualize the interactions.

See the audience clapping because they enjoyed you speak.

The audience was engaged.

They understood your clear message and were inspired to action (depending on the purpose of your talk).

Visualize the entire process of you having delivered your talk with impact from start to finish.

You Aced it.

Repeat this visualization process as many times as you can.

Your mind doesn't distinguish fact from fiction.

When it's time for action, your subconscious mind will be saying, *"Hey, this looks familiar. We've been here before. I know exactly what to do. Let's rock and roll"*.

"There are always three speeches, for every one you actually gave. The one you practiced, the one you gave, and the one you wish you gave."

Dale Carnegie

40 STAND UP. SPEAK!

The likes of Martin Luther King, Winston Churchill and John F. Kennedy captured the imagination of their audience, their people and their nation.

They delivered their message in a way that made themselves and their message memorable.

You too can do the same, no matter who you are, and what position you're in.

I mention these 'Greats' because they started from a place that was all too familiar to most of us.

Martin Luther King (MLK) reached and resonated with his audience not by just merely reading words. He gave *life* to them. He touched people's hearts and minds.

This came with practice. MLK received a "C" in his public speaking class in college.

Winston Churchill (WC) inspired a nation. Unbeknown to many, he wasn't a gifted speaker. He spent hours, days and weeks on end practicing and refining his speeches.

If you must know, WC would suffer from sweaty palms and bouts of tears when preparing for his talks. He also stuttered.

John F Kennedy (JFK) worked hard to become a man that symbolizes a great public speaker. That came with practice, coaching and effort.

JFK was a man whose hands and knees would *shake* early on in his career.

The common thread about these *Great Speakers* is that they took the time to develop and refine their public speaking skills into an art form.

You too can do the same.

Coaching, effort, focus, knowledge, practice- *forever*.

This book has given you plenty to begin with.

You can only get better, deliver better and feel better through action.

Let your message be heard. Speak!

"Become so good that they will

have to notice you"

Steve Martin

ON A SCALE OF 1 TO 10

HOW DO YOU NOW FEEL ABOUT

YOUR PUBLIC SPEAKING ABILITY?

1   2   3   4   5   6   7   8   9   10

Not too confident   Complete Confidence

CAN WE HELP YOU AND YOUR GROUP?

Voice Projection

Body Language

Speech Writing

Presentation Skills Training

Sales Presentation Training

Public Address Training

Stage Skills

Media Training

Shadowing

TYPE OF SERVICES INCLUDE

In-person boutique one on one training

Executive Communication and Leadership Coaching

Private workshops for groups

Crisis Management

Communication Consultancy

Bookings Enquiries:

Info@KevinAbdulrahman.com

"Developing excellent communication skills is absolutely essential to effective leadership.

The leader must be able to share knowledge and ideas to transmit a sense of urgency and enthusiasm to others.

If a leader can't get a message across clearly to motivate others to act on it, then having a message doesn't even matter."

Gilbert Amelio